CLASSICAL MUSIC

FOR BEGINNERS

Written by Stacy Combs Lynch
Illustrated by Michael D. Lynch

WRITERS AND READERS PUBLISHING, INC.
P.O. Box 461, Village Station
New York, NY 10014

Writers and Readers Limited
9 Cynthia Street
London N1 9JF
England
•

A Writers and Readers Documentary Comic Book
Copyright © 1994
Library of Congress Catalog Card Number: 94-61222
ISBN # 0-86316-162-6 Trade
2 3 4 5 6 7 8 9 0

ML
240
.L96
1994

Manufactured in the United States of America

Beginners Documentary Comic Books are published by Writers and Readers Publishing, Inc. Its trademark, consisting of the words "For Beginners, Writers and Readers Documentary Comic Books" and the Writers and Readers logo, is registered in the U. S. Patent and Trademark Office and in other countries.

Writers and Readers—
publishing FOR BEGINNERS™ books
continuously since 1975:

1975: Cuba • 1976: Marx • 1977: Lenin • 1978: Nuclear Power • 1979: Einstein • Freud • 1980: Mao • Trotsky • 1981: Capitalism • 1982: Darwin • Economists • French Revolution • Marx's Kapital • French Revolution • Food • Ecology • 1983: DNA • Ireland • 1984: London • Peace • Medicine • Orwell • Reagan • Nicaragua • Black History • 1985: Marx Diary • 1986: Zen • Psychiatry • Reich • Socialism • Computers • Brecht • Elvis • 1988: Architecture • Sex • JFK • Virginia Woolf • 1990: Nietzsche • Plato • Malcolm X • Judaism • 1991: WW II • Erotica • African History • 1992: Philosophy • Rainforests • Malcolm X • Miles Davis • Islam • Pan Africanism • 1993: Psychiatry • Black Women • Arabs & Israel • Freud • 1994: Babies • Foucault • Heidegger • Hemingway • Classical Music • 1995: Jazz • Jewish Holocaust • Health Care • Domestic Violence • Sartre • United Nations • Black Holocaust • Black Panthers • Martial Arts • History of Clowns • 1996: Opera • Biology • Saussure • UNICEF • Kierkegaard • Addiction & Recovery • I Ching • Buddha • Derrida • Chomsky • McLuhan • Jung • 1997: Lacan • Shakespeare • Structuralism

CLASSICAL MUSIC
FOR BEGINNERS

Contents

Congratulations!

You've already passed the first hurdle by actually picking up a book with the words "Classical Music" in the title. But why are those two harmless words so scary? What exactly are you afraid of? Fear of inadequacy? Fear of boredom? Fear of clapping at the wrong time? Let's examine those fears one by one.

1 Fear of inadequacy —

Guess what?

You know more classical music than you think. Ever watch Bugs Bunny or the Smurfs on Saturday morning cartoons? Then you're familiar with tunes from Rossini's operas *The Barber of Seville* and *William Tell,* Wagner's epic music drama *The Ring of the Nibelung,* Grieg's *Peer Gynt* suite, Rimsky-Korsakov's *Scheherazade* and Strauss' tone poem *Till Eulenspiegel.* And TV advertisers are always sneaking in a bit of Bach or Beethoven to help sell a product (which makes good sense, dollar-wise, since many classical works are in the public domain, meaning anyone can use them and you don't have to pay royalties). And hit movies such as *Platoon, The Four Seasons* and *Ordinary People* helped introduce the works of Barber, Vivaldi and Pachelbel to millions who would never have heard them otherwise.

So relax. It's not as foreign as it seems. You'll be humming along in no time.

2 Fear of boredom —

Well, there's a chance that could happen.

But did you know that the average opera will expose you to more sex, murder and deception than a week's worth of the TV soaps (they *are* called "soap operas")? And often there is unintended humor in the form of a two-hundred pound soprano singing about how she's wasting away from tuberculosis or unrequited love. Plus, the occasional "surprise" or "musical joke" (from Haydn and Mozart, respectively) to keep you on your toes.

3 Fear of clapping at the wrong time—

There are two things you can do.

Either don't go to live concerts or clap when everyone else claps. You aren't alone — 90% of the people at any given concert are waiting for someone else to clap first; the other 10% are just showing off for the rest of us.

$\mathcal{S}$o, we've established that there's nothing to be afraid of, right? And as you acquaint yourself with a composer and his works it will become even less scary. (Sorry, though women served as, er, "inspiration" for quite a few important works, there are no female composers represented here — blame the times please, not the author!) Presented here then, as an introduction to the world of "serious" music, are the lives, historical eras and works of twenty-four major composers.

You just may discover a new passion or a favorite composer.
At the very least, you can impress your friends during the next round of Jeopardy!

Before we start, I have a question for you. . .

What Exactly IS Classical Music?

Classical =
"of the highest rank,"
"having lasting
significance."

Classical **music** =
"distinguished from
popular or folk music."

*W*hen we in the West say "Classical music,"
what we are referring to would be more accurately
described as "music composed in the European
tradition from the Baroque Era (beginning roughly
1600) through the early 20th century."

$\mathcal{M}$usic didn't just happen in 1600.
And Western civilization didn't invent it.

Every culture has had its own music.

As language skills developed, people used music as a way of passing history down from generation to generation.

Isn't it easier to memorize the words to a song than to memorize a poem or a story?

𝒜nd different cultures developed their music in different ways...and for different purposes:

As a form of worship

To make work pass more quickly

To accompany soldiers off to war

In fact, much of Western classical music developed out of music written for religious services and sacred rites. Then, of course, the kings and dignitaries, who saw themselves as "god-like," wanted their own specially written music. Maybe that's why classical music is often (wrongly) perceived as "elitist" — something that "ordinary people" wouldn't be interested in.

As music became more complex, a system for recording it on paper became necessary.

By the 10th century, a system of notation had developed that is similar to that which is used today.

Around 1600 — during what is called the Baroque Era — European composers began to write the first music that we now consider "classical."

There is no great mystery to reading music, and it is not difficult to learn.

See the *"Intermission"* on page 116 for a brief and basic lesson.

What Is This Book's Focus?

An introductory book on classical music could focus on many things, from a broad historical overview (*e.g.,* the Renaissance, the French Revolution) to specific musical compositions (*e.g.,* Handel's *Messiah*, Beethoven's Fifth Symphony).

This book focuses on neither of those things. (One is too wide; the other is too narrow.)

CLASSICAL MUSIC FOR BEGINNERS focuses on the **composers** themselves — *and* on the **Musical Eras** in which they worked. Beginning with the Baroque Era and continuing through the early 20th century, CLASSICAL MUSIC FOR BEGINNERS presents twenty-four of the most influential and popular composers of Western classical music, taking note of their genius and their flaws, and explaining what made them great and what kept them human.

The composers are discussed in chronological order, with a brief introduction to the musical era in which they lived and worked. To help readers discover favorites of their own, the most important and/or popular works of each composer are listed at the end of each section — along with occasional "*Intermissions*" to clarify/explain specific terms, such as the Symphony Orchestra, the Conductor, etc.

The book is divided
into four Musical Eras:

The Baroque Era: 1600 to 1750

The Classical Era: 1750 to 1820

The Romantic Era: 1820 to 1900

The Post-Romantic Era: 1890 to 1930

(the above dates are rough approximations)

STOP!!!...and make a
distinction between
"Classical" <u>music</u> (*all* of the
music discussed in this book)
and **The "Classical"** <u>Era</u> (from
1750 to 1820).

THE Baroque Era

- ❂ Bach
- ❂ Vivaldi
- ❂ Handel

Intermission
CHAMBER MUSIC

The Baroque Era

The musicians and composers of the Baroque Era did not think of themselves as "Baroque." That label was applied years later by guys trying to get Ph.D.s, who studied the music of the past and concluded that between approximately 1600 and 1750 (roughly the same period as the Baroque Era in art) the majority of music being composed had in common a particular style that differentiated it from the music that came before and after those dates.

Baroque = Ornate, flambouyant, elaborate, richly ornamented.
Baroque **Music** = marked by strict forms and elaborate ornamentations

What is it that makes a piece of baroque music Baroque? Basically, four things:

Grand Passions

Contrast

Playing Freedom against Structure

Ornateness — truckloads of Ornateness

Composers of the Baroque Era tried to convey through their music, grand passions and deep thoughts such as heroism, ecstacy, reverence, or self-sacrifice. These passions were not necessarily those of the Composer (this was before people believed that an artist must do his own suffering in order to create), but rather an attempt to show, through contrast, the widest possible range of ideas and feelings.

The juxtaposition of

FREEDOM & STRUCTURE

was the single-most distinguishing feature of the era.

That and the ornateness. (Maybe you've heard of "minimalism;" Baroque was "maximalism.")

Freedom aside for a moment, there were many rules and formulas that governed Baroque composition and a composer had to be well-schooled in "theory," the "mathematical" formulas that dictated how to write a piece of music. The Baroque grand passions and deep thoughts had, through centuries of use, become "codified" so that if a composer wanted to express "reverence," he knew just what notes to put together to get that effect.

This is not as mysterious as it may seem. If you were asked to describe "Jingle Bells" and "The Battle Hymn of the Republic," you'd probably say one is happy and carefree while the other is heroic and sad. Through repetition and refinement, our ears have come to recognize some sounds as one thing and some as another.

n the other hand, Baroque music was more than just a math problem — it was the way in which a composer worked within or around those rules (*or even broke them*) that made one composer an artist and another a mere calculator.

Think of it this way: If there are no rules, then any person (or monkey, or computer) could put any bunch of notes together and call it music. (And himself a composer!) It is the ability to use limitations creatively that separates "art" from "formula."

Baroque music had its rules and structure and a composer showed his artistry within those limits, but there were often also whole sections of improvisatory "free" passages that a composer only suggested to the performer through the barest outline such as a **recitative** (a style of vocal music that imitated the rhythms of speech) or a **fantasia** (an improvised solo instrumental piece). Classical musicians of today shy away from improvisation, but in the Baroque Era a performer had to be skilled at it.

The musical blueprint could also be affected through the use of **ornamentation**, which means exactly what it sounds like: a simple melody made "frilly" through the use of various **trills** (a fast fluttering between two notes) and **turns** (playing the note above and below the principal note before finally landing on the actual written note).

The use of ornamentation not only allowed a performer to show off his or her skill, it was also *functional*, because some musical instruments of the time (the harpsichord, for instance) were incapable of sustaining a note — so ornamentation basically filled up the space between notes.

During the Baroque Era, composers began writing music with a particular instrument in mind — a violin or oboe, for example — and tailoring the pieces to fit the technical capabilities and tone color of that particular instrument. Even so, music was often played once and then discarded. The music of the Baroque was constantly changing, never static, and often a surprise.

Johann Sebastian Bach

(1685-1750)

During his lifetime, the German composer Johann Sebastian Bach wrote thousands of compositions and fathered some twenty children. Today, Bach is considered one of the greatest composers of all time, and his music is revered as the culmination of the Baroque Era.

Oddly enough, though he was highly regarded as a virtuoso organist, Bach was neither rich nor famous during his lifetime. He spent most of his career as a church musician and many of his greatest works were composed specifically for church services and functions.

I AM ONE OF THE GREATEST COMPOSERS OF ALL TIME

JUST GIVE US SOMETHING THE CHOIR CAN SING!

BUT IF IT AIN'T BAROQUE I DON'T FIX IT!

As a young man, Bach taught himself certain styles of composition by copying out by hand the works of composers he admired. He also frequently made changes he thought would improve the originals.

$\mathcal{L}$ike most of the top musicians of his day — and like jazz musicians of today — Bach was an expert at improvisation, making up music on the spot. It was not considered disrespectful to the composer for a musician to add ornaments, trills or **cadenzas** (an extended solo passage near the end of a piece, allowing a performer to show off his technical and improvisatory skills).

TAKE THAT RIFF, BABY. MAKE IT SING!

Sadly though, because music was often composed on the spot, it was not always preserved on paper. Even those compositions that were written out were often not considered worth saving. Music written for a certain event was often discarded after it was performed. There was no need to save it — old Bach could easily whip off another. So even though more than one thousand of Bach's compositions have survived, it is staggering to think of those we'll never hear.

Bach was a deeply religious, God-fearing man, and in many of his choral works one hears the ecstatic joy and solemn reverence he felt toward the Almighty. His settings of the "Passions" according to St. John and St. Matthew are superb examples of highly dramatic story-telling, utilizing soloists, chorus and orchestra. These works were the closest Bach came to writing an opera. (Opera existed in Bach's time but had not yet enjoyed its heyday).

Some of Bach's most famous works are those entitled "Toccata and Fugue."

Toccata = a Baroque composition for organ or other keyboard instrument, intended to show, teach or show-off "touch."
Fugue = a Baroque musical form in which a theme is stated, repeated, then developed contrapuntally.
Counterpoint = two (or more) melodies played at the same time that sound good together (technically, they "establish a harmonic relationship").

The opening notes of Bach's Toccata and Fugue in D Minor are familiar to TV and movie fans as "Dracula's Theme," or "haunted house music."

MAJOR & MINOR KEYS: If you're not a musician, the most useful way to think of "Keys" is in terms of their effect on the listener: Major Keys sound happy; Minor Keys sound sad.

Toward the end of Bach's life he composed the *Art of the Fugue,* in which one fugue subject (or theme) is treated eighteen times, each more complex and detailed than the last, yet each adhering to the same rigid structure. It is considered a masterpiece of musical architecture.

Another set of "Preludes and Fugues" was the *Well-Tempered Clavier.* ("Well-tempered" doesn't refer the good-humor of the instrument, but to a method of tuning that has survived to this day.) The *Well-Tempered Clavier* progresses through all keys, major and minor, and the pieces are often used as "**etudes**" (teaching pieces used to develop technical skill), resulting in ill-tempered young music students everywhere.

Other notable compositions include The Brandenburg Concerti, the B Minor Mass and a *Musical Offering*, dedicated to Frederick the Great of Prussia, who had suggested the theme to Bach.

Add to these, countless cantatas, sonatas, suites, concerti and chorales ...

When did this guy ever find time for twenty children?!!

Antonio Vivaldi
(1678-1741)

NOW IT'S MY TURN.

The Italian composer Antonio Vivaldi studied both music and for the priesthood before finally deciding upon music as his profession. Nicknamed the "Red Priest" because of his religious leanings and his red hair, Vivaldi was employed for most of his adult life as teacher, composer and conductor in a school for orphaned and illegitimate girls in Venice. Many of the children were accomplished musicians so, Vivaldi had at his disposal a stable of ready musicians on which to try out his newest works.

(Which he turned out by the dozens.)

Vivaldi's music was very popular during most of his lifetime until late in his life when he fell out of favor with the public. He was quickly forgotten by the musical world after his death and was only rediscovered when researchers found that Bach had admired his work.

Whatever the circumstances of his "rediscovery," Vivaldi occupies a well-deserved place in music history through his refinement of the **concerto** form.

CONCERTO: a piece of music written for a solo instrument, or group of instruments, accompanied by an orchestra and usually set in three movements: fast, slow and fast.

Though he wrote all types of music, it is the concerto that he is most remembered for (though not always positively — one critic accused him of writing the same concerto 500 times), and many of the more than 500 concerti that he composed are performed today, most particularly, the *Four Seasons* (familiar from its frequent use in TV and film).

WORK TO KNOW
The Four Seasons

George Frideric Handel

(1685-1759)

German-born George Frideric Handel is the composer of one of the world's best-known pieces of music: the "Allelujah" chorus from his oratorio, *Messiah*.

DID YOU KNOW?
According to some traditions, you are supposed to stand when the "Allelujah" chorus is sung.

YES, BUT...DO YOU KNOW WHY?
King George II inadvertently started this tradition at a performance of the *Messiah* in London. When the chorus began the "Allelujah" section, the king was so bowled over it literally brought him to his feet. His faithful subjects followed suit and the tradition has continued to this day.

WOOO!
THAT'S GREAT!
YEAH!

Ironically though, Handel's main interest was always in writing opera. In fact, we are lucky the *Messiah* was ever composed at all because Handel's parents were more interested in a law career than a music career for young George Frideric. But music lessons began at an early age and compositions soon followed.

Music! Music! I don't understand it, son! Stop playing that piano—here's a briefcase and tie—you're going to study law!

Handel, like Bach, taught himself certain styles of composition by copying the works of composers he admired — in Handel's case, the Italian opera composers. He eventually realized that in order to really learn the style, he would have to live and study in Italy, where he became well-versed in the operatic style and achieved considerable success. He later moved to London, where he became a citizen and stayed the rest of his life.

But Handel ran into problems in London. His operas were serious and heroic, but his largely middle-class, not overly educated London audience was tiring of this old form: they wanted to hear the newer comic-operas. Handel knew that he had to find a subject matter they could relate to.

Except for the fact that they were not allowed to be performed in theatres, biblical texts were ideal. Handel solved this problem by presenting the stories in the form of **oratorios** and performing them not in theatres, but in concert halls.

Do You Know the Difference Between. . ?

Opera: staged, acted, performed in a theater.

Oratorio: also dramatic (tells a story), but just sung, not acted. The subject matter is usually sacred, though not written to be performed during a church service. In common: drama, showcase for virtuoso singers.

OPERA

ORATORIO

And since Handel was not writing opera — a form that was considered "Italian" (and therefore the **libretto**, or words, were written in Italian) — he was able to write his oratorios in English, which certainly made them more accessible to an English-speaking audience.

I SAY! NOW I SEE WHAT THEY'RE GOING ON ABOUT!

$\mathfrak{H}$is oratorios and other works were successful; Handel lived a comfortable but low-keyed life. Largely neglected after his death, his works are now frequently performed, and he is recognized as the great dramatist he wished to be.

WORKS TO KNOW
Messiah   Water Music
Judas Maccabeus   Fireworks Music

Just about the only thing he didn't write was **Chamber Music.**

Chamber Music

Chamber music is music that is written for small groups of instruments or voice — usually two to ten players — with one player on a part (meaning there is not a section of twenty violins all playing the same music), and no conductor. The size of the ensemble makes this music suitable for more intimate settings — such as a private home or the king's official "chambers" — than that of a symphony orchestra. (That's why we call it "chamber music.")

WHERE TO PERFORM CHAMBER MUSIC

HERE: NOT   HERE:

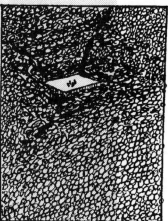

G

iven this broad definition, chamber music has probably existed since man discovered harmony and first accompanied a voice with an instrument. Before the days of mass entertainment, many priviledged Europeans played an instrument, and families often gathered for fun and music-making, utilizing whatever instruments were handy and playing the "popular" tunes of the day.

As composers began writing music for specific instruments and the parts became more and more complex, chamber music began to loose its "amateurish" or "just-for-fun" status. Haydn and a handful of other composers (Boccherini and Scarlatti, for example) helped push the form into the "big leagues" of serious music.

Haydn's works for string quartet earned him the nickname "father of the string quartet."

THE Classical Era

- *Haydn*
- *Mozart*
- *Beethoven*

Intermission
THE SYMPHONY

The Classical Era

The term "classical music" has never been a satisfactory one for the music this book discusses, partly because that one term is used to mean two different things: *all* "classical" **music** and the "Classical **Era**" in music. But that is the term that is commonly used, so we're pretty much stuck with it.

We will continue to use "Classical music," generically, to mean all types of "serious" music discussed in this book while pointing out that the "Classical Era" was the period of approximately seventy years following the Baroque. Both usages probably came about from attempts to distinguish what was thought of as "classic" (of highest rank, or having lasting significance) from all the rest.

Dates for the Classical Era are generally accepted to be 1750 to 1820. Keep in mind that these dates are approximate. Obviously, the Baroque didn't end neatly one day, everyone deciding to be Classical from then on. There were definite overlaps between the two periods (as with all historical eras), with Baroque tendencies pushing on into the Classical Era and some late Baroque music that could even be called "pre-Classical." But there were differences.

*T*n the era that followed the Baroque, ideas about music changed with the evolving political thought. The rise to prominence and power of the middle class brought on by the French and American Revolutions, brought with it the democritization of the arts and of learning. Music publishing expanded to include amateurs who were hungry for music they could learn easily; concerts were now open to the public rather than exclusively for royalty or the well-to-do.

This new interest in the arts combined with dwindling royal patronage (kings used to keep "stables" of musicians ready to create and perform new works for any occasion), necessitated music that was accessible to many; not just to those listeners who had studied formally.

$\mathcal{M}$usic in the Classical Era sought to meet these new listeners on their own levels, to please and entertain, not to astonish or cause undue mental strain (you weren't supposed to have to *think* about music). The Classical Era appreciated "good taste" rather than passion or poetry, and universal truths above national interests.

The music, like the age, was humanitarian, striving to please all. The "ideal" music would encompass the best qualities of the music of all nations. Music of the Classical Era was purged of what was seen then as Baroque pretense and grandeur.

Franz Joseph Haydn

(1732-1809)

> W·E·L·L·LL! MR. HAYDN, YOUR SON IS ONE TALENTED CHOIR BOY AND HE COULD KEEP THAT LOVELY SOPRANO VOICE...

Franz Joseph Haydn began his musical training as a young child and was a choir boy in Vienna. His voice was so good that, as one story has it, he was told it would take only a "simple operation" to keep his lovely, boyish voice forever. Young Haydn was all for it, but his father quickly vetoed that idea. Haydn's parents weren't all that keen on his becoming a musician at all. They wanted him to become a priest. At least a clergyman made a steady living.

> ...IF HE HAD A SIMPLE OPERATION!

> OPERATION?

DID YOU KNOW. . ?
Yes, there really was such an operation. From the 16th century through Haydn's time, castrated males (the **CASTRATI**) were very popular on stage, performing the roles that were forbidden to women by the church. The practice had pretty much fallen out of favor by Haydn's time.

*H*aydn did become a musician, and as a young man was hired as assistant to the music director of the Esterhazy (nearby Hungary's powerful noble family) court. The patronage of the royal family was quite a coup for the young Haydn and his parents were no doubt thrilled that he had a steady job, not to mention ready musicians on whom to experiment and try out his new works.

His popularity became so great, in fact, that publishers were not beyond putting his name on pieces of music that he had no part in composing — because they knew any piece written by Haydn would sell. Because of this fraud, it is not known exactly how many pieces of music Haydn wrote.

What *is* known is that he wrote more than 100 symphonies and nearly as many string quartets.

HISTORICAL NOTE—It's still happening: In December 1993, the music world heralded the discovery of six "lost" piano sonatas by Haydn, suddenly "found" in Germany. Deemed "Haydnesque" by a number of musicologists and musicians (who no doubt, wanted it to be true), they were later found to be fakes!

41

$\mathcal{I}$t was not through numbers alone that Haydn achieved his fame. With his string quartet compositions, he legitimized a form of music that had been looked upon as mere "parlor music" — music that amateurs might play for fun; entertaining perhaps, but not serious. It took Haydn to recognize the potential of a group of four instruments from the same musical family, to hear their musical capabilities expressed through this intimate kind of music. He influenced later composers of quartet music, and his own quartets are still very popular today.

(See the *"Intermission"* on CHAMBER MUSIC on page 33.)

*M*any of the 100-plus symphonies that Haydn wrote have been given nicknames (but not by Haydn); for instance "The Clock", whose tic-toc rhythm reminds the listener of a you-know-what, and the "Surprise Symphony" in which a loud chord, suddenly and seemingly out of place, wakes up any audience member who may have drifted off to sleep.

SURPRISE SYMPHONY VICTIMS

Surprises or not, Haydn was a uniquely "classical" musician who dedicated himself to his craft and labored to develop it throughout his life. His works are free of Baroque "pretension"; they achieve the very purity that Classical composers strove for.

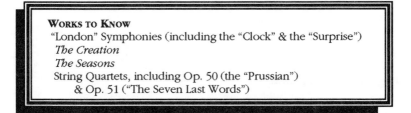

WORKS TO KNOW
"London" Symphonies (including the "Clock" & the "Surprise")
The Creation
The Seasons
String Quartets, including Op. 50 (the "Prussian")
& Op. 51 ("The Seven Last Words")

Wolfgang Amadeus Mozart

(1756-1791)

olfgang Amadeus Mozart was born into a musical family in Salzburg, Austria, where he began his musical studies —to say the least— at an early age. Recognizing his son's prodigiousness, the elder Mozart abandoned his own musical career and devoted all his time to the education and career of his young son. Papa Mozart was the ultimate "stage mom."

WAAAAAAH!

MY SON! THAT'S A PERFECT "C"!

*D*uring Mozart's time, performers, if they were lucky, belonged to a royal court, where they were considered little more than servants. Mozart's early years were spent touring, entertaining the kings and queens of Europe with musical tricks such as sight-reading difficult pieces, improvising long pieces of music from a short melodic theme or playing an instrument with the keys covered by a handkerchief.

$\mathscr{M}$ozart was more than a charming and precocious child; he was also an immensely talented musician and composer. He composed his first works before the age of six and wrote a full symphony before his ninth birthday.

As a young man, Mozart, like his father, was employed by the Archbishop of Salzburg, who provided a steady but oppressive living for the young composer. After several years he resigned the post and moved to Vienna, where he was finally out from under his father's thumb. Anticipating a busy free-lance career as performer, composer and teacher —especially after the success of his opera, *The Abduction from the Seraglio* (set in a Turkish harem), Mozart spent and entertained lavishly. Against his father's wishes, he married Constanze Weber, the sister of a woman he had been infatuated with.

*M*uch of Mozart's music was composed on commission for a particular occasion — garden parties, birthdays, home concerts, etc. But while he was composing constantly — operas, symphonies, chamber music — the commissions were never enough to pay the costs of Mozart's lavish lifestyle. The debts piled up.

Dying young (age thirty-five), poor, and unappreciated is the stuff legends are made of, and legend surrounds the history of Mozart. One story has it that he could compose whole pieces of music right out of his head while doing something as innocuous as playing billiards. And how could someone who could write music like *that*, have been so amused by bathroom humor and dirty words, as his letters indicate?

And, of course, there is the mystery of his untimely death: What killed Mozart? Infection? Exhaustion? Rival composer Salieri?

FACT OR FICTION? Those who have seen the movie or stageplay *Amadeus*, based on Mozart's life, are familiar with this theory. Though it made for a great drama — and Salieri himself claimed to have poisoned Mozart!— there is no evidence that it was true. The rumor, however, has persisted for years.

*B*ut while the details of Mozart's life and death are still the subject of dispute, there is no dispute over the fact that he was one of the greatest composers of all time.

WORKS TO KNOW

Operas:	"Jupiter" Symphony, K. 551
Don Giovanni	"Prague" Symphony, K. 504
The Abduction From the Seraglio	"Haydn" string quartets
The Marriage of Figaro	Clarinet Quintet, K.581
Cosi Fan Tutte	"Coronation" concerto for piano, K. 537
The Magic Flute	

Ludwig Van Beethoven

(1770-1827)

A giant among musical giants, Beethoven stands alone in the history of music, with ties to both the classical and romantic periods, yet really belonging to neither.

CHOOSING UP SIDES

49

orn in Bonn, Germany to an established family of musicians, young Beethoven was pushed by his father to become a child prodigy practically from the cradle.

COME ON SON! YOU'RE FIVE YEARS OLD! TIME TO COMPOSE AN OPERA!

I BEETHOVEN, AM A GENIUS!

YOU'RE INCORRIGIBLE!

MR MOZART

MR SALIERI

MR HAYDN

But though his training started early and his talent was apparent, he never became the famous child star that Mozart was. Still, he studied with the best teachers, encountering along his way, Mozart himself, Haydn, and Salieri, among others.

His teachers, quick to admire his abilities, were also quick to denounce the impetuous streak and fiery temperament that showed not only in his personality, but in his music. Indeed, it is impossible to separate Beethoven, the man, from his music. And it is Beethoven we see when we think of an "artist" — that tortured, idealistic figure, fist raised in defiance to the gods.

*D*espite his great talent, composition was never easy for Beethoven. His original manuscripts show innumerable inkblots, revisions and other signs of frustration. Beethoven was a perfectionist. He was always his own worst critic, while at the same time, fully aware that he was a great artist.

BEETHOVEN DISAPPOINTS
BY LUDWIG VAN BEETHOVEN
ONCE AGAIN I DO
NOT LIVE UP TO MY
EXPECTATIONS...

And he was. More than any other composer up to that time, Beethoven was able to take many seemingly different musical ideas and moods and *make* them make sense together. His music was not always pretty. Beethoven was more concerned with truth.

I DON'T LIKE YOUR MUSIC

MY MUSIC IS FOR A LATER AGE

CRITIC

While Beethoven's music may have been harsh and disturbing to some, it was nonetheless popular. After settling in Vienna, Beethoven, unlike Mozart, established himself as a "free agent." He didn't have to depend on a royal court for his living, so he could compose and perform as he wished. In this way (and in others), Beethoven was an innovator, always ahead of his time. He seemed to know this: in reply to a critic who didn't think highly of his work, Beethoven replied that his music was "for a later age." History seems to have borne him out.

*B*eethoven began to go deaf in his early twenties. His hearing declined steadily. He was completely deaf in his later years. Although this helped contribute to the image of a suffering artist that the romantics so admired — and Beethoven himself suffered frequent bouts of depression over the loss of his hearing — his *music* never suffered. His output never diminished.

It is perhaps because he lived and composed without the reality of sound, that he was more attuned to sound as an *abstraction*, and was thus able to use it without the biases and limitations of his time, pushing the limits of what was musically acceptable.

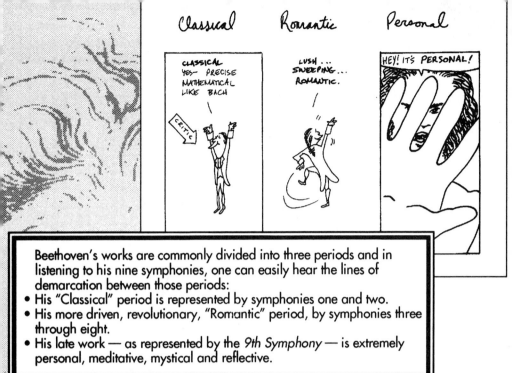

Beethoven's works are commonly divided into three periods and in listening to his nine symphonies, one can easily hear the lines of demarcation between those periods:

- His "Classical" period is represented by symphonies one and two.
- His more driven, revolutionary, "Romantic" period, by symphonies three through eight.
- His late work — as represented by the *9th Symphony* — is extremely personal, meditative, mystical and reflective.

*H*istory has never really recovered from Beethoven. Today, we accept without question that an artist must "express himself," that he is misunderstood and ahead of his time. But in his time, Beethoven was a radical. He took the Classical form as far as it could go, destroyed its simplicity and demanded a new musical language to deal with his ideas. And if the history of music is a process of evolution, then Beethoven's work led inevitably to the Romantic Era.

WORKS TO KNOW
Opera: *Fidelio*
The nine symphonies
Piano Concerto No. 5 in E flat major ("Emperor")
Piano Sonata in C minor ("Pathetique")
The late string quartets
Mass: *Missa Solemnis*

INTERMISSION

The Symphony

Just as a composer can write an opera, a piece of chamber music or a song, he or she can also write a **Symphony.** Originally, a symphony was an **overture**

(the music already playing before the curtain rises, just in case you were stuck in traffic and arrived a little late) to an opera.

But since Haydn's time, it has become a serious orchestral work, much longer than an overture.

*W*ritten obviously for the instrumentation of the symphony orchestra, the way in which it is written (its **form**) follows a strict set of guidelines.

Without going into details, a symphony generally consists of three or four sections called **movements** which are in contrasting mood or tempo, usually

FAST — SLOW — *FAST*, or

FAST — SLOW — a *DANCE*-like *rhythm* — *FAST*.

And that is exactly what those fancy names — "allegro" (fast), "adagio" (slow), etc. — that appear in the concert program mean.

HINT: If you know how many movements there are in a piece of music, and you have an idea of the "style" of each, you'll know when the piece ends. And when to applaud!

The Romantic Era

- Schubert
- Schumann

Intermission
THE VIRTUOSO

- Mendelssohn
- Chopin
- Liszt

Intermission
ITALIAN OPERA

- Donizetti
- Rossini
- Verdi
- Puccini

Intermission
THE SYMPHONY
ORCHESTRA

- Berlioz
- Tchaikovsky
- Brahms
- Wagner

Intermission
THE CONDUCTOR

The Romantic Era

Although the Romantic Era in music lasted from approximately 1820 to the end of the century, our 20th century view of art is still very much colored by romantic thought. The music of this era is probably the most accessible to our 20th century ears, particularly to the new listener. It is from the romantics that we get such ideas as the timelessness of art, that art is without boundaries, is yearning, political, and that an artist is expressing his or her own personality through the work of art.

And although these things are probably somewhat true of all periods in music, it is the romantics who took them as their battle cry in what they saw as a revolt against the constraints and limitations of the Classical Era.

Romantic composers and other artists envisioned a new sort of art in which different artistic forms would take on characteristics of the others — poetry would become musical, music would become poetic. This led to what the romantics called **program music** — instrumental music that suggested a story or concept.

Composers wanted to express through instrumental music the "states of being" that they saw as beyond words and music. They often sought to portray dreamlike states: the supernatural, mystical, subconscious levels of the mind. It was perhaps a reaction to the industrial revolution and the great advances in scientific knowledge that sent artists in search of these "spiritual truths," and led inevitably to the extensions of harmony, melody and orchestral color necessary to express them.

Composers of the Romantic Era had a rather strange and contradictory relationship with their audiences.

Music was no longer for the exclusive enjoyment of royalty and the upper classes. The rise to prominence and greater earning (and therefore, buying) power of the middle class meant a huge potential audience for music. It also meant reaching an audience that was probably unschooled in music performance, let alone theory.

So, while a romantic composer yearned to "enlighten," if he wanted to eat, he'd better also entertain. From this contradiction came the concept that an artist was a suffering genius, misunderstood and unappreciated in his own time, writing for a mythical "ideal audience" that would understand his works.

Franz Schubert

(1797-1828)

Viennese composer Franz Schubert was born in 1797, one of fourteen children; he died thirty-one years later of syphilis (which was incurable at the time) complicated by typhoid fever. During those thirty-one short years, he composed more than 600 lieder, nine symphonies, fifteen string quartets, several song cycles, tons of piano music and quite a few operas.

Schubert studied composition with the Italian composer, Salieri, the contemporary and "rival" of Mozart. He later took up teaching as a way to avoid the military.

NUMBER 597.
NUMBER 598,...
HERE YOU GO!

LIEDER = a German word meaning "songs", and referring to a specific kind of romantic composition for voice, accompanied by a piano.

Like any good romantic composer, Schubert idolized Beethoven. He was a coffin-bearer at the great composer's funeral and once remarked to a friend who had complimented his own work, "Who can do anything after Beethoven?" Schubert was buried — at his request — near the grave of his idol.

Although Schubert is now considered nearly as great a composer as Mozart or Beethoven, during his lifetime he never knew fame and was nearly always poverty-stricken. Though he wrote several operas, none were successful and most were never even staged. The first six of his nine symphonies were written for an amateur orchestra, but the symphonies considered his greatest (the 9th), and his best-known (the 8th, or "Unfinished"), were not performed during his lifetime. And though we now know that he wrote many works for piano, very few of these were known (much less performed) during his lifetime.

This is partly due to the fact that Schubert, a decent pianist, was not a fiery **virtuoso** and did not have the sort of performance career in which he could promote and perform his own music.
(See *"Intermission"* on page 65 for a brief rundown of **Virtuoso.**)

UH, MAYBE IT'LL BE READY NEXT WEEK...

To make matters worse, he was not a good businessman. The works that he did manage to sell made him very little money, though they somehow managed to make a tidy sum for his unscrupulous publishers.

But Schubert was a popular man, if not a popular composer, and his many friends helped him through the lean times. For entertainment, Schubert and his arty friends would meet in cafes for an evening of dancing, singing and the performance of Schubert's latest works. These events were nicknamed "Schubertiads" and were perhaps the nineteenth-century equivalent of the poetry readings, performances and happenings of the 1950s/60s "coffee-house scene."

Though his operatic works never quite caught on, Schubert had no rivals as a song-writer, for which he seemed uniquely gifted. His melodies were strong and he had a great feeling for harmonic color. Schubert gave the piano a more important role in his music. Equal musically to the voice part, the pianist was often called upon to create the "mood" of the piece, or to "paint" the musical picture, and the piano part was written to complement the text itself.

Schubert is now well-regarded for his works for string quartet and other chamber ensembles. Among the greatest are his "Trout" Quintet for Strings and Piano and his C major Quintet, written for string quartet plus an extra cello. His symphonies, as well, are widely performed, attesting to his well-earned popularity in the 20th century.

WORKS TO KNOW
Symphony No. 8 in B minor ("Unfinished")
Symphony No. 9 in C major ("The Great")
Piano Quintet in A major ("Trout")
String Quartet in D minor ("Death and the Maiden")
Song Cycles: *Die Schone Mullerin, Die Winterreise, Schwanengesang*

Robert Schumann

(1810-1856)

German composer Robert Schumann was the next great composer of lieder (German art songs) after Schubert. Schumann was interested in both poetry and music, which is reflected in many of his compositions. His piano accompaniments are themselves musically interesting, more a duet between voice and piano than soloist and accompanist. His works for the piano are not easy, but neither are they show-off pieces. Schumann never subordinated the "poetry" of the music to virtuosic displays.

When Schumann was a young man, he fell in love with his piano teacher's daughter, Clara, who was herself a musician and was being prepared by her father for a career as a virtuoso pianist. Against her father's wishes, the two eventually married.

Schumann had also hoped for a virtuoso performing career — perhaps in order to assure that his own works were performed — but a rather ridiculous finger injury ended that dream. The story of Schumann's injured finger is an opera in itself: some say that he had rigged a kind of sling device that he wore while practicing in order to isolate and strengthen the fourth finger of his right hand; others maintain that a venereal disease crippled his finger (!!??); and some say he simply practiced too hard. Whatever the reason, he did not become the virtuoso that he had hoped. (Maybe it was because he strengthened the wrong hand.)

It is now assumed that Schumann was a manic-depressive. During his manic periods he turned out incredible compositions and founded a newspaper of musical criticism, serving as its editor and introducing Chopin and Brahms among others, to the musical world.

But Schumann's great highs were countered by severe bouts of depression — he once tried to commit suicide by jumping off a bridge in Dusseldorf into the Rhine. His depression became so overpowering that he spent his last years in an asylum, where he was visited faithfully by his wife and their friend Johannes Brahms — who was, himself, in love with Clara!

Clara continued her career as a teacher and performer for many years after her husband's death and was a great champion of his works, dressing for all her concert appearances in "widow's black."

Though Schumann's life and works were typically romantic, he seemed to realize the dangers of romanticizing tragic events and anti-social behavior. In a diary he wrote, "The artist should beware of losing touch with society. Otherwise, he will be wrecked, as I am."

WORKS TO KNOW
Symphony No. 1 in B flat major ("Spring")
Songs: *Dichterliebe, Frauenliebe und -Leben*
Piano works: *Papillons, Phantasiestucke*

The Virtuoso Performer

*The need to win the approval — for monetary, if not spiritual reasons — of a huge number of people gave rise to another Romantic Era phenomenon: the **virtuoso** performer. The fiery fingerwork and crowd-pleasing feats of seeming magic provided an audience with the entertainment it wanted and provided the performer, often also a composer, a chance to gain popularity.*

Unfortunately, it also deepened the gulf between the professional and amateur musician.

Three of the most famous piano virtuosos of all time were Mendelssohn, Chopin and Liszt.

Felix Mendelssohn-Bartholdy

(1809-1847)

Although German composer Felix Mendelssohn lived a short life, by all accounts it was a serene and happy one — not exactly the life of a good romantic!! His music, like his life, though somewhat influenced by romanticism, was never overwhelmed by its excesses. He was a virtuoso pianist and his music requires a great technique, but it is always elegant — never virtuosic for virtuosity's sake.

Like Mozart, Mendelssohn was a child prodigy, giving his first public concert at the age of nine. He composed part of the music for one of his most famous works, "A Midsummer Night's Dream," when he was only a teenager; the famous scherzo and the even more famous "wedding march" (yes, **that** wedding march) came some sixteen years later.

HE'S ALWAYS LIKE THIS WHEN HE GETS BACK FROM A TRIP.

A great "painter" of romantic landscapes through music, Mendelssohn was heavily influenced by his travels and Scotland seems to have particularly struck him, resulting in the "Hebrides" overture and the "Scottish" (third) Symphony. Likewise, a trip to Italy produced the "Italian" (fourth) Symphony.

Prestigious conducting positions in Leipzig and Dusseldorf rounded out Mendelssohn's successful career, though Germany's prevalent anti-semitism (Mendelssohn was Jewish by birth, but a convert to the Protestant faith) denied him others.

WORKS TO KNOW
Incidental music for "A Midsummer Night's Dream"
Symphony No. 3 in A minor ("Scottish")
Symphony No. 4 in A major ("Italian")
Piano and Violin concerti
Piano Collection: "Songs Without Words"

Frederic Chopin

(1810-1849)

Polish-born Frederic Chopin wrote almost exclusively for the piano. The favored instrument of the Romantic Era, the piano had undergone technical refinements (from wood to a metal frame, for one), and Chopin is credited with expanding the instrument's "musical" and "poetic" capabilities.

Though his musical talent was evident from an early age — a work he composed at the age of seven had gained public notice — he was introduced to the music world as a young man by Robert and Clara Schumann, who pronounced him "a genius."

Chopin's native Poland inspired many of his works (including the "Mazurkas" and "Polonaises"), foreshadowing the "nationalism" trend that would take over musical Europe later in the century. Other important works include the "Nocturnes," "Impromptus" and "Preludes" and several sets of "Etudes".

Chopin lived most of his life in Paris, where his company was sought out by members of Parisian "high society" who wanted to show him off in their salons. A somewhat effeminate man, he had a ten-year relationship with the suit-wearing, cigar-smoking, female novelist who called herself George Sand,

> proving that opposites do, indeed, attract.

Works to Know
(all for piano)
Three Nocturnes, Op. 9
Three Nocturnes, Op. 15
Polonaises, Mazurkas, Waltzes

... NOW WITH MUSICAL, POETIC, SINGING QUALITIES!

CALL NOW! IT'S ALL HERE ON THE HOME CHOPIN CLUB!

HCC

BOOoooooo BOoooooo BOoooooooooo!

Franz Liszt

(1811-1886)

T he Hungarian, Franz Liszt, was
(like Mozart) a child prodigy who
toured Europe, performing "tricks" and
astounding audiences. His parlor tricks made young Franz the idol of
Paris (the Paris Opera commissioned a work from him when he was just
thirteen!), and his popularity and talent persuaded several noblemen to
provide tuition for his study in Vienna, the musical capital of Europe.

Later a true virtuoso of
the piano, the adult Liszt
was able to use his
power as a performer to
persuade listeners to
accept "new music." If
Brahms was the
conservative of the
romantic movement,
Liszt was its radical.
Accordingly, he was a
great champion of
Wagner's music, and the
two were good friends
— which worked out
quite well when Wagner
married Liszt's daughter,
Cosima.

Liszt divided his time between his performing career in Paris and his career as composer/conductor in Weimar, Germany. Somewhere in all that, he even found time to take Holy Orders in Rome. Paradoxically though, Liszt had been involved in a series of love affairs including one with a married countess with whom he eventually lived and had several children (one of whom was Cosima).

His best-known works are probably the "Hungarian Rhapsodies" for piano and the "Transcendental Studies," the latter written when he was just a teenager but considered one of the masterpieces of piano literature.

WORKS TO KNOW
Hungarian Rhapsodies
Transcendental Studies

INTERMISSION

Italian Opera

By now, you may be thinking that all classical music originated in Germany or Austria. True, Germany dominated the *instrumental* music world and had done a decent job adapting Italian Opera to serve German purposes. But for centuries the Italians had been refining and perfecting their national treasure — Italian Opera.

Italy was not as susceptible to the romantic movement as Germany, nor was its music as experimental. To the Italians, the opera was about human drama and should have realistic plots instead of the mythology and symbolism favored by the Germans.
Italian opera should delight and move its audience. It should be popular.

Experimental or not, opera is still automatically associated with Italy, and many of its best-loved classics were composed by the gentlemen included here:
**Donizetti,
Rossini,
Verdi and
Puccini.**

73

Gaetano Donizetti

(1797-1848)

Born to a non-musical family (his father was a weaver) that did not like the idea of his becoming a musician (so what else is new?), Italian-born Gaetano Donizetti joined the army as a young man — not in order to see the world, but because he thought he would have time to devote to composition and receive an income at the same time.

Perhaps it was this grabbing a moment here and there that earned him his reputation for composing works at record speed. He once jokingly scoffed at the composer Rossini for taking *a whole two weeks* to compose his opera, *The Barber of Seville!*

D onizetti, himself, composed some 70 operas, most notably *Lucia di Lammermoor, Don Pasquale* and *L'Elisir d'amore (The Elixir of Love).*

Not one to overstay his welcome, Donizetti admitted toward the end of his life, "My heyday is over. I am more than happy to cede my place to people of talent." He died of syphilis.

WORKS TO KNOW
Operas:
Lucia di Lammermoor
Don Pasquale
L'Elisir d'amore

Gioacchino Rossini

(1792-1868)

Τ
he principal Italian composer of the early 19th century, Rossini was born in the town of Lugo to a local musician who also worked as an inspector of slaughter houses. Both of his parents were involved in a theater group, which Rossini himself joined as a teenager; excellent training for the future opera composer.

He quit the formal study of music at the age of seventeen when his teacher told him that while he didn't know enough about composition to write church music, his knowledge was sufficient for opera.

His teacher was correct at least as far as opera was concerned. Rossini had great success, was celebrated in London and Paris, and was commissioned by La Scala and other theaters to write two operas per year.

ROSSINI'S DAYTIMER:

1812 (age 20)

MON finish sonata	TUE compose opera
WED revise overture	THU start etude
FRI pull all-nighter	SAT / SUN

Describing himself as "congenitally lazy," he might be better described as someone who "worked hard and played hard." He composed most of his works between the ages of eighteen and thirty, and contented himself during the second half of his life with living well and entertaining lavishly. Considering food as important as music, Rossini said that he knew "... no more admirable occupation than eating — really eating."

During those few productive years, he produced thirty-two operas, two oratorios, symphonies, cantatas and many other works, including his masterpiece of grand opera *Guillaume Tell (William Tell)* whose overture everyone knows as the "Lone Ranger" Theme.

WORKS TO KNOW
The Barber of Seville
William Tell
The Italian Girl in Algiers
La Gazza Ladra
Semiramide
LaCenerentola (Cinderella)

ROSSINI'S DAYTIMER:

1832 (age 40)

MON Party	TUE Party
WED Party	THU Party
FRI Party	SAT Party / SUN Party

Guiseppe Verdi

(1813-1901)

The great Italian opera composer, Guiseppe Verdi, was turned down from the Milan Conservatory in his youth because his piano playing wasn't considered up-to-par. This son of a tavern-keeper continued his studies nonetheless, and eventually composed some of the best — and best-loved — works in the operatic repertoire.

ALTHOUGH WE **DIDN'T** ACCEPT YOUR ADMISSION TO THE CONSERVATORY TWENTY YEARS AGO, WE WERE WONDERING IF MAYBE - NOW THAT YOU'RE **FAMOUS** YOU'D CONDUCT ONE OF YOUR OPERAS FOR US?

DEAN

THANK YOU FOR COMING MR. VERDI!

Milan Conservatory

Though the Italians weren't as seduced by Romanticism as were the Germans, Verdi had his share of pain. His wife and two young children died tragically and Verdi found it nearly impossible to go on. Though he was under contract at the time to compose a comic opera, he vowed never to compose again. But he did compose again, perhaps due in part to his falling in love with a singer whom he later married (but not until after they had lived together for ten years — causing great scandal among his neighbors).

Verdi lived a long life and was for a while involved in politics, working for a united Italy until his political life overtook his life as a composer. He finally gave up politics and came back to the opera world with one of his masterpieces, *Aida*.

V erdi was not an experimenter or an innovator like Richard Wagner, his goal was perfecting the art-form of his countrymen. That so many of his twenty-six operas have withstood the test of time — including *La Traviata, Rigoletto, Il Trovatore* and *Aida* — shows to what degree he succeeded. Not all of his works were instant successes, however: *La Traviata*, now an operatic classic, was an absolute failure at its first performance. Asked whether he thought the opera's failure was his own fault or that of the singers, Verdi answered prophetically, "Time will tell."

It did. His death, at age eighty-seven, was an occasion of national mourning for Italy, so great was his prestige and popularity.

WORKS TO KNOW

La Traviata	*Aida*
Rigoletto	*Il Trovatore*
Falstaff	*Otello*
Requiem for four voices, choir and orchestra	

Giacomo Puccini

(1858-1924)

Giacomo Puccini came from a family of musicians. Going along with the family tradition, he first took up the organ as his instrument — but after hearing the works of Verdi, Puccini decided that he must devote himself entirely to the opera. Puccini ultimately became opera's most important Italian composer in the late 19th and early 20th century.

GIACOMO, MY SON — I'M TELLIN' YOU, YOU'RE FUTURE'S AS AN **ORGANIST!**

FAMOUS Composer's School

His unabashed sentimentality and sense of melodrama have made *La Boheme, Tosca* (her famous cry: "Love and music, these have I lived for.") and *Madame Butterfly* (though at its premiere, it was booed off the stage) classics of the operatic repertoire and influenced the works of such modern musical theatre composers as Andrew Lloyd Webber of *Phantom of the Opera* and *Cats* fame.

Puccini's last opera, *Turandot,* was incomplete when he died. Though one of his students completed the work faithfully, at its premiere, the famous conductor Toscanini, stopped the performance where Puccini had stopped writing. He turned to the audience, and said,

"HERE, DEATH TRIUMPHED OVER ART."

WORKS TO KNOW
La Boheme
Tosca
Madame Butterfly
Turandot

INTERMISSION

The Symphony Orchestra

When most people think of "classical music," the symphony orchestra comes immediately to mind: one hundred musicians in formal attire, bows gliding simultaneously; a frantic, wild-haired conductor directing traffic from a podium up front. This is classical music at its most visible.

But the symphony orchestra as we think of it today only came into being in the mid-18th century — not so long ago, really, considering music's ancient past — and even then there was no conductor.

WHAT'S THAT GUY DOIN' UP THERE?

$\mathcal{S}$omething similar to the symphony orchestra had existed even in the time of Bach and Handel. Conducted from the vantage point of the keyboard, it generally consisted of strings, flutes, oboes, trumpets, trombones, harpsichord and other instruments as needed (often, whatever instruments were available), the strings being the "core" of the group.

By Beethoven's time, the Symphony Orchestra had expanded to just about what it is today:

STRINGS — consisting of violins, violas, cellos, and basses;

WOODWINDS — flutes, oboes, clarinets and bassoons (often complemented at the top and bottom registers with piccolo, English horn, E-flat and bass clarinets and contra-bassoon);

BRASS — trumpets, french horns, trombones and tubas;

PERCUSSION — consisting of various drums (timpani, snare, bass, etc.), cymbals, tambourine, xylophone and many other inventive percussive sounds, as necessary.

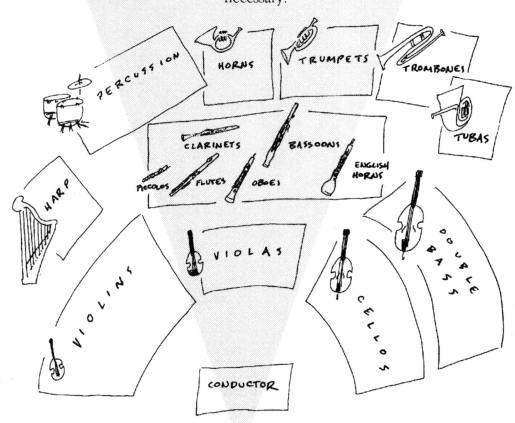

The French composer Hector Berlioz is credited with establishing the orchestra's definitive instrumental groupings.

Hector Berlioz

(1803-1869)

The Frenchman Hector Berlioz was yet another musician whose parents wanted for their son a more stable career. He was actually enrolled in medical school before deciding to turn all his efforts to music. His parents needn't have worried, though, because their son Hector became an important composer, an influential critic and is considered the founder of modern orchestral conducting.

His works are famous for their literary influences and "programmatic" aspects (meaning they tell a story) and for their complex orchestration. Being a conductor, Berlioz had an orchestra at hand to experiment on and eventually came up with the definitive groupings of instruments into sections (strings, brass, winds, percussion). He also wrote several important works on orchestration.

ORCHESTRATION = adapting music to the orchestra in such a way as to achieve the desired effect in terms of timbre, loudness, balance, etc.

Berlioz' ideas on orchestration met with some resistance from the conservative musical establishment. This was in part due to the fact that he was not a pianist (his instruments were guitar and recorder—a kind of flute), and the old guard couldn't believe that he would even try to compose orchestral works without a background in piano. But he proved that it was unnecessary.

Berlioz supplemented his composing and conducting income by writing articles and reviews, a task he hated (but at least it kept his parents from worrying).

Berlioz' best-known work is the *Symphonie Fantastique*. Originally sub-titled, "Episodes in the Life of an Artist," the work was composed after his proposal of marriage was turned down by his lover. (Later, she did marry him, and then, once his beloved was attained, he cheated on her.) The "story" of the piece involves opium-induced hallucinations in which a man pursues the woman he loves; each hallucination growing more and more strange, finally ending in a witch's orgy.

WORKS TO KNOW
Oratorio: *La Damnation de Faust*
Romeo et Juliette, a symphonic drama for soloists, chorus and orchestra
Opera: *Benvenuto Cellini*
Symphony Fantastique
For viola and orchrstra: *Harold in Italy*

Peter Illyich Tchaikovsky

(1840-1893)

Russian composer Peter Illyich Tchaikovsky is probably best known as composer of the music for the Christmas ballet classic, *The Nutcracker*. He also composed music for the ballets, *Swan Lake* and *Sleeping Beauty*. A "late bloomer", Tchaikovsky didn't begin serious musical study until he was in his twenties and had a career as a civil servant up to that time.

Though he is not regarded by most music scholars as an innovator, his music is among the most popular in the symphonic repertoire, even today. Tchaikovsky, though a Russian (and the first Russian composer to attain worldwide popularity), was heavily influenced by the German romantic movement, and his music is as full of angst and theatrical displays of emotion as that of any German composer. In addition to the ballets, popular works include the last three of his six symphonies, the piano concerto in B-flat minor and the violin concerto.

Since art imitated life in the Romantic Era, one could assume correctly that Tchaikovsky's life was also filled with angst and emotion. His one marriage lasted no more than a few days. Never comfortable with his sexuality, the marriage was no doubt a feeble attempt to deny his homosexual proclivities.

Though the marriage was an utter failure, Tchaikovsky did have a strange, yet intimate relationship with an aristocratic woman who became his patron.

Though they lived in the same city and she provided him with a salary, the two never met, preferring in-depth correspondence by mail, rather than meeting face-to face.

Tchaikovsky died at a fairly young age. The long-accepted version of his death was that he contracted cholera after drinking contaminated water but now scholars say he was ordered to commit suicide to avoid scandal over his sexual advances to a young man.

WORKS TO KNOW
Symphonies 4-6
Ballet Music: *Swan Lake, The Sleeping Beauty, The Nutcracker*
Piano Concerto No. 1 in D minor
Violin Concerto in D major

Johannes Brahms

(1833-1897)

The popularity and accessibility, even today, of the music of Johannes Brahms — considered a "conservative" of the romantic movement — proves that one need not be on the cutting edge of art in order to appeal to a later age.

CUTTING EDGE COMPOSERS

BRAHMS

I'M A ROMANTIC REBEL!

OH YEAH! CRAAAAZY MUSIC IS MY GAME!

MR ESTABLISHMENT THAT'S ME.

CARD CARRYING CONSERVATIVE J. Brahms

Brahms' works were lush, expressive and beautiful, while at the same time, tightly controlled: classic in construction, romantic in sound, yet very individualistic. He was not of that school of "spontaneous inspiration" that the romantics held so dear — his ideas were carefully thought out, and he consciously tried to avoid those things he saw as "pitfalls" of the romantic movement.

I JUST
HAD A
SPONTANEOUS
IDEA FOR
A SYMPHONY

HEY!
ME
TOO!

NO NO NO NO
NO NO NO NO
NO NO
SAY NO TO
SPONTANAIETY!

Brahms, who was born in Hamburg, Germany, came from a cultured, if somewhat offbeat (for its time) family: His mother was seventeen years older than her husband, and, by all accounts, wore the pants in the family; his father was an accomplished musician but haphazard provider for his family.

His parents did see, however, that young Brahms received a solid education in music, languages and poetry, if not material comforts. They divorced when Brahms was a young man. Brahms took a job playing the piano in a tavern when he was in his early teens.

Though modest and socially ill-at-ease, Brahms' immense talent was apparent enough to inspire enthusiastic supporters. As a young man he was introduced to Robert and Clara Schumann, who befriended him and helped advance his career. Brahms, who never married, carried a life-long torch for his friend, Mrs. Schumann.

During his day, Brahms was considered the leader of the musical camp that opposed the forward-looking music of Richard Wagner. And though he actually signed a manifesto against this "new music," the rivalry with Wagner was something he did not seek, for he admired Wagner's works greatly. Nevertheless, he was looked upon by many of his contemporaries as a link to the past: his first symphony was often referred to as "Beethoven's Tenth" — at once a compliment and a condemnation (and a fact that must have infuriated Wagner, who saw himself as Beethoven's heir).

Though they may not have been sufficiently ground-breaking to satisfy the Wagnerites, Brahms' works — hundreds of lieder, the four symphonies, four concerti, piano works, chamber music — have survived as some of the best-loved and most often performed in the repertoire. Not bad for a guy who never wanted to call attention to himself.

WORKS TO KNOW
Symphonies 1 - 4
Haydn *Variations*
Violin Concerto in D minor
Double Concerto in A major for violin & cello
A German Requiem
String Quartets   Clarinet Quintet

Richard Wagner

(1813-1883)

Richard Wagner, born in Leipzig, Germany, was arguably opera's greatest composer.

"ARGUABLY?"
WHO SAID THAT?
BRAHMS?!

Beethoven
CONCERT
TONITE

IF **HE** CAN DO IT, **I** CAN DO IT!

In fact, one of the world's best-known melodies — "Here Comes the Bride" — is from his opera, *Lohengrin*. Although interested in many intellectual pursuits — politics, philosophy, debate — Wagner (according to legend) decided on a career in music after hearing the works of Beethoven.

Career decided upon, he quickly came up against a roadblock: To Wagner, Beethoven's music was as perfect as had ever been written. What could Wagner say that Beethoven had not already said? ?

His solution was something that he called "the art of the future," which he envisioned as a combination of all the arts — music, drama, dance, painting, poetry, etc. This combination, as Wagner saw it, was possible only through opera, which he called "music drama."

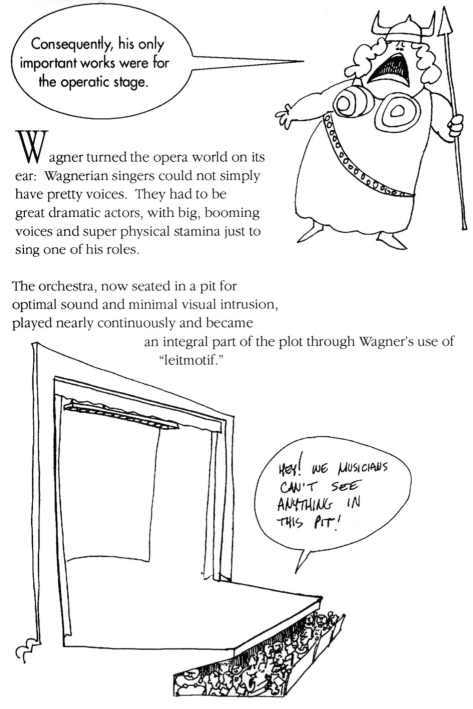

Consequently, his only important works were for the operatic stage.

W agner turned the opera world on its ear: Wagnerian singers could not simply have pretty voices. They had to be great dramatic actors, with big, booming voices and super physical stamina just to sing one of his roles.

The orchestra, now seated in a pit for optimal sound and minimal visual intrusion, played nearly continuously and became an integral part of the plot through Wagner's use of "leitmotif."

HEY! WE MUSICIANS CAN'T SEE ANYTHING IN THIS PIT!

Sets, costumes, lighting — all were important to Wagner and he designed one of the world's most famous opera houses — the "Festspielhaus" (Festival Theater) in Bayreuth, Germany — as the ideal setting for his "art of the future." His many innovations revolutionized the way opera was presented.

LEITMOTIF = a short melody that, through repetition, became associated with a particular character or event. These tiny "theme songs" were a musical nudge to both audience and on-stage characters, reminding them of important events or specific characters not present at the time.

Wagner was a thinker and an innovator. He was also opinionated and outspoken — scandal seemed to follow him everywhere. He lived for ten years in Switzerland after fleeing Germany to avoid being arrested for political crimes. He was constantly in debt and he had a well-earned reputation as a womanizer.

I even married the wife of my best friend (the slightly weird daughter of Franz Liszt). After a lengthy affair under her husband's nose, Cosima Liszt vonBulow left the oblivious fool to be with me--to whom she often referred to as "the Master."

But Wagner's music must stand alone. While many had, and continue to have, problems with Wagner the man, the continued popularity of his works attest to his greatness as a composer. Wagner may have thought there was nothing more to be said musically after Beethoven, but it is he who pushed the music of the time to its very limits and helped to usher in the modern age and modern, atonal, music. He truly was an innovator.

W agner is often linked with the philosopher Friedreich Nietzsche. The two did admire each other for a time but later broke off their friendship. Wagner's music (and no doubt, his political leanings and revolutionary spirit) and Nietzsche's writings were apparently inspirational (though it can be argued that both were taken out of context) to Nazi Germany decades later. Because Hitler idolized Wagner and his music was often played in Nazi concentration camps, Wagner's music is not often performed in Israel even today — scandal still follows him after a century.

WORKS TO KNOW
. . .all operas. . .

Parsifal	*The Flying Dutchman*
Tannhauser	*Lohengrin*
Tristan and Isolde	*The Mastersingers of Nuremburg*

The Ring of the Nibelungs:
— a cycle of four operas/music dramas —
(The Rhine Gold, The Valkyries, Siegfried,
The Twilight of the Gods)

INTERMISSION
The Conductor
What does he actually **do?**

The conductor does not play an instrument or perform a thrilling solo. Nor is he or she the one that missed the note, or came in at the wrong time. So who is this person and why does he or she get the credit — or the condemnation — for what the orchestra does?

Looks like he's just up there waving a little stick, right? Well that's probably his main job — waving the stick. But each one of those waves means something. There are patterns he must follow depending on the "beat" of the music — if he skips a beat or forgets and starts conducting the pattern for "four beats to a measure" instead of "three beats to a measure," the whole orchestra is off.

Imagine trying to get 100 temperamental musicians — each with his or her own idea of how the piece should go — to agree on anything at all. That's another part of conducting — being able to "lead" the orchestra through a piece of music, controlling balance (telling the trumpets to play softly so the audience can hear the clarinet), adjusting intonation (being able to hear, while all the other musicians are playing their parts, that the "C" in the second violins and the "A" in the oboe are a hair off) . . .and getting the orchestra to play the way her ear dictates the piece should sound.

Knowing how the piece should sound and being able to communicate that to the orchestra is what separates the women from the girls (and the studs from the duds) in the world of conducting. First, she must thoroughly know the "score" — her "map" of the piece of music, with each line of music for each instrument. She must know that while the flutes are playing this, the double basses are playing that, and that the horns make their entrance in the next measure. She must have hundreds of such pieces — some lasting more than an hour — stored in her brain.

But more than good memorization skills, the conductor must, like any instrumentalist, have a sense of "musicality" — a combination of drama, emotion, taste, creativity, knowledge and technical skill. He must convey his "interpretation" to the instrumentalists so that they are playing the way he wants them to. He conveys this with his gestures, his body language, his face, his eyes and his baton. When a conductor is performing, every facial twitch and bead of sweat mean something.

The conductor cannot be shy. He must involve the audience as well as the musicians. He cannot run his orchestra as a democracy. He has full dictatorial power. A brilliant conductor is revered. A mediocre conductor is despised.

POST-ROMANTICISM
& the Early 20th Century

* *Mahler*
* *Debussy*
* *Strauss*
* *Stravinsky*
* *Shostakovich*

Intermission
READING MUSIC

Post-Romanticism and the Early 20th Century

(...Or, after Wagner, then what?)

Romanticism didn't end suddenly on a certain date or even at the beginning of the 20th century. Scholars generally refer to the late 19th century as "Post-Romanticism." Wagner, who died in 1883, had exploited romanticism for nearly all it was worth. And while all this was going on, other "isms" were popping up as well; these were what brought music into the 20th century.

A sense of "nationalism" — or national pride — had been taking hold for some time. Composers were growing dissatisfied with the German and Austrian dominance of the music world and began doing things their own ways, using folk tunes, dances and tales from their own homelands. Exponents of the "new" national styles were Czech composers Bedrich Smetana and Antonin Dvorak; Finnish composer Jean Sibelius; the Norwegian Edvard Grieg; Russians Dimitri Shostakovich, Modest Mussorgsky and Sergei Prokofiev; Ralph Vaughn Williams and Gustav Holst from Britain; and the American, Aaron Copland.

But that's not all ...

Following trends in art, some composers (most notably, two Frenchmen, Claude Debussy and Maurice Ravel) wrote in a style called "Impressionism," which sought to create a mood or an atmosphere, rather than telling a story. Bucking that trend, others wrote in a style called "Expressionism" (Arnold Schoenberg and Alban Berg — both Austrians), which represented the "inner" experience of man in the modern world: isolated, helpless and torn by conflict. Schoenberg's "atonal" school of composition was a huge influence on later 20th century composers — and is blamed by many for the "collapse" of melody, and the end of "music you can hum".

(Though definitely a major figure in the history of music, Schoenberg, even today is an acquired taste, more popular with historians and musicologists than with listeners. Readers who can't resist a challenge should check out his *Pierrot Lunaire*.)

Except for Schoenberg, new listeners will have no problems with most of the music of this "post" romantic period. So revolutionary for its day, time has eroded much of its so-called harshness.

Gustav Mahler

(1860-1911)

*T*hough the music of Bohemian-
born Gustav Mahler is very much in
fashion, during his lifetime he was more
famous as a conductor — leading among others, the New York Philharmonic
(he was paid the highest salary in the orchestra's history up to that time:
$30,000 per year) and the Metropolitan Opera. Most of his works were
composed during the summer, between conducting seasons.

Though Mahler was a celebrated conductor, he was not happy merely
interpreting the works of others but it was an economic necessity after his
parents and sister died, leaving him with the task of supporting his five younger
brothers and sisters. Mahler was rather stoic about the situation, echoing the
Romantic sentiment that, "People will only realize what I am when I am gone."

By Mahler's time, works for the symphony orchestra were getting longer and
longer and calling for more and more performers. Mahler's works were typical
of this Post-Romantic period, several of his symphonies lasting more than
eighty minutes. His Eighth Symphony, scored for soloists, organ, huge chorus
and orchestra, is aptly named "Symphony of a Thousand."

*H*is most important work is probably the song-cycle, *Das Lied von der Erde* (The Song of the Earth). Evident here is the Post-Romantic trait of weaving a sense of deadly foreboding through music of sumptuous beauty and ecstatic pleasure, as if to say, "enjoy it while you can". To Mahler, each work was "a world" in itself: sophistication juxtaposed with simplicity, cosmic ideas next to folk tunes.

Mahler and Freud had a "famous" conversation during which they concluded that Mahler's need to counter a profound thought with something comical came from hearing his parents argue as a child, running outside to escape and hearing a hurdy-gurdy (a crank organ) being played in the street. From then on, Mahler associated tragedy with comedy.

Mahler's works, in many ways, are the epitome of the romantic movement. He took many of the traits of romanticism as far as they could legitimately go and he took music to its tonal limits. (In some of Mahler's music the ear cannot easily find a tonal center, its "home plate." If you imagined a church hymn stopping before the "amen" is sung, it would sound unfinished. That's because the amen returns the music to its main note, or the "tonic" of its key. In Mahler's music, it was often impossible to find this "main note.")

WORKS TO KNOW
Symphony No. 1 in D major
Symphony No. 2 in C minor
Symphony No. 8 in E flat major
Song cycle: *Songs of a Wayfarer, The Song of the Earth*

Claude DeBussy

(1862-1918)

*A*lthough French composer Claude Debussy wrote in several different styles, he is most often associated with the "Impressionist" movement. Like its counterpart in the art world, Impressionism in music sought to blur lines and create a mood (rather than a specific, detailed picture) through the use of varied tone colors and harmonies. Debussy's most famous work in this style is the *Prelude a l'apres midi d'une faune* (Prelude to the Afternoon of a Faun). The piece, typical of many of Debussy's works, calls for a large orchestra, but seldom calls upon it to make a big sound.

Born to a family of farmers, Debussy enrolled at the Paris Conservatory at the age of eleven. He scandalized many of his teachers by daring to question the accepted rules of composition, but his disdain was simply following a trend of rejecting organized structure that had already happened in literature and art. Debussy was further inspired after a trip to Russia, where he encountered the works of the composer, Mussorgsky (most famous for his *Pictures at an Exhibition*), whose musical ideas regarding form, structure and imagery paralleled Debussy's.

WORKS TO KNOW
Symphonic sketches: *La Mer* (The Sea)
Prelude to the Afternoon of a Faun
Opera: *Pelleas and Melisande*

Though he was quite a revolutionary for his time, his music no longer sounds strange to our ears. His influence was felt in the music of every significant composer since that time and he was soon recognized as the composer who "liberated" French music from Germanic influence.

But as strange as his music may have seemed in the late 19th and early 20th century, Debussy had his admirers, even then. He said of the so-called Debussyites, who formed a kind of artsy cult, that they would end up "disgusting" him with his own music.

Richard Strauss

(1864-1949)

*B*orn in Munich, Germany, Richard Strauss became famous for his "tone poems," which were symphonic works based on well-known themes from literature or folklore. Strauss' tone poems include *Macbeth, Tod und Verklarung (Death and Transfiguration*, whose romantic subject was the progression of the soul through suffering to transcendence), *Don Quixote, Till Eulenspiegel* (the story of the legendary trickster) and his most public work, *Also sprach Zarathustra*, based on the poem by philosopher Friedrich Nietzsche, and known to nearly everyone as the music from the movie *2001: A Space Odyssey.*

Strauss also wrote a tone poem called *Ein Heldenleben* (A Hero's Life), a supposedly autobiographical work about his struggles against the hostile critics of his music. Unsurprisingly, he received lots of criticism for that bit of self-indulgence.

But Strauss was quite sure of his powers of musical expressiveness and communication. To him, all good music must tell a story. He once told a colleague, "I can translate anything into sound. I can make you understand by music that I pick up my fork and spoon from this side of my plate and put them down on the other side." Whether or not his powers were quite that great, he did find some redemption on his deathbed, when he told his daughter that death was just as he had composed it (in *Death and Transfiguration*).

Other important works by the composer include the operas *Salome, Elektra* and *Der Rosenkavalier* (The Cavalier of the Rose).

Igor Stravinsky

(1882-1971)

*E*ven though Russian composer Igor Stravinsky's parents were themselves musicians, they persuaded him to prepare for a more practical career in law before he realized that music was indeed his calling. His early influences were Russian composers Tchaikovsky and Rimsky-Korsakov, who persuaded the young musician to try his hand at composition.

Stravinsky became an international star at a young age after the impresario Serge Diaghilev (at Rimsky's persuasion) commissioned him to compose music for his ballet company, the most famous of these works being *La Sacre du Printemps* (The Rite of Spring). Harsh-sounding and full of dissonance and pounding rhythm, it is an erotically charged piece about pagan rites and the appeasement of the gods. Probably the most important work of its time and now an accepted part of the symphonic repertoire (the ballet, however, did not fare as well as the music), the *Rite* was considered so outrageous at its 1913 premiere in Paris that it caused a riot.

$\mathcal{S}$urprisingly enough, the composer of arguably the most important work of the 20th century went through a neo-classical phase. Not that he started composing in the style of Mozart or Haydn, but Stravinsky adapted a "classical" form to his own unique voice — absolutely counter to what was going on in the rest of the musical world. Later in his life, he became interested in the twelve-tone technique, a completely new method of composition devised by the Austrian composer, Schoenberg. He apparently wanted to test his skills against any set of rules.

Still, Stravinsky had a somewhat Baroque attitude toward composition. He said of his feelings on composing: "The more art is controlled, limited, worked over, the more it is free .... My freedom will be so much the greater and more meaningful the more narrowly I limit my field of action and the more I surround myself with obstacles .... The more constraints one imposes, the more one frees oneself of the chains that shackle the spirit."

WORKS TO KNOW
(from the Stravinsky/Diaghilev collaboration)
The Rite of Spring, *The Firebird* and *Petrushka*
(first performed by the famed dancer, Nijinsky)
Opera: *L'histoire du soldat* (The Soldier's Tale)
Oedipus Rex

Dmitri Shostakovich

(1906-1975)

Shostakovich was much-touted as the "first Russian composer after the Revolution," and even his earliest works were political (*e.g.* "Funeral March for Victims of the Revolution"). Born in St. Petersburg, Russia, his first symphony was performed to great acclaim while he was still a student and was added to the repertoirs of several of the world's orchestras.

Later on, when he was well-established at home and abroad, he fell out of favor with the Soviet government and its newspaper, *Pravda*, which attacked his works as "too modernistic" and a "triumph of noise over melody." From that time on, his music was either "in" or "out," depending upon the current political climate.

Soviet art, at that time, had to appeal to the masses and could not be tainted by "bourgeois decadence" or a surplus of "intellectualism." Shostakovich tried to comply with what the party wanted, subtitling his fifth symphony, "A Soviet Artist's Reply to Just Criticism." Still, he was deemed, "an enemy of the people." Though his music had been officially censored, when the government needed him (he was known throughout the world), he was "uncensored" and sent on "goodwill" missions as a musical ambassador, an act of hypocracy that he hated.

Works to Know
Symphony No. 5 in D minor
Symphony No. 10 in E minor
Piano Quintet

A Brief Lesson in Reading Music

There is no great mystery to reading music.
Here is how it works:

Each note is represented by a letter of the alphabet...

A B C D E F G

Notes are written on a "staff" of five lines, each line and each space between the lines representing a specific note.

Reading the staff from bottom to top, the notes are:

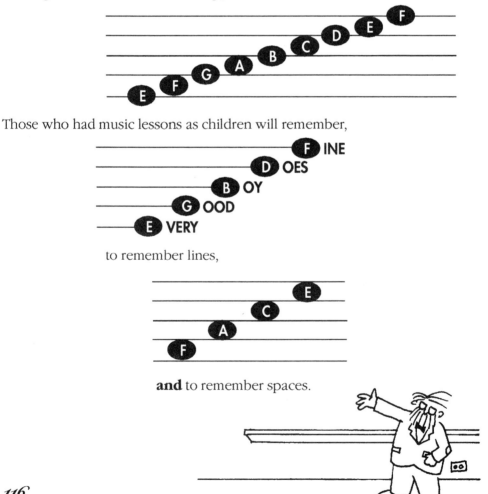

Those who had music lessons as children will remember,

F INE
D OES
B OY
G OOD
E VERY

to remember lines,

and to remember spaces.

Notes can also exist above and below the staff and are indicated by "leger lines." Keep counting the lines and spaces up or down in the A-G sequence to determine the name of a note.

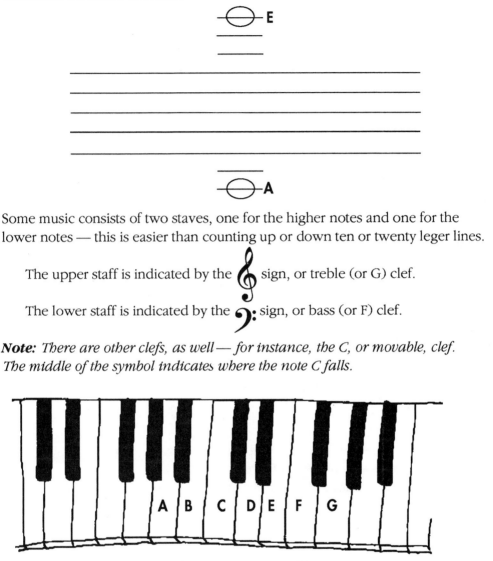

Some music consists of two staves, one for the higher notes and one for the lower notes — this is easier than counting up or down ten or twenty leger lines.

The upper staff is indicated by the 𝄞 sign, or treble (or G) clef.

The lower staff is indicated by the 𝄢 sign, or bass (or F) clef.

Note: *There are other clefs, as well — for instance, the C, or movable, clef. The middle of the symbol indicates where the note C falls.*

A, B, C, D, E, F, and G are the white notes on a piano keyboard.
The black keys on the piano are the "in-between" notes:
The note between C and D is called either C-sharp (♯) or D-flat (♭).
A sharp ^raises a note while a flat _lowers it.

In other words, the ♯ (sharp) sign written in front of the note C, tells the player to raise that note to the pitch that falls between C and D.
A ♭ (flat) sign written before the note D, tells the player to lower that note to the pitch that falls between the D and the C.

The staff is divided into measures, or bars, by vertical lines. A measure can be filled with any combination of notes and rhythms —

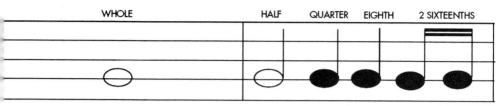

one long note (a "whole" note, filling up the "whole" measure),

or many fast notes (fractions of a whole note —half, quarter, eighth, sixteenth, etc.), but the amount of time the measure occupies is the same.

A "meter" or "time" signature is indicated at the beginning of the staff. It consists of two numbers, one written above the other —for example 3/4. The top number, **3**, indicates that the piece of music is divided up into measures that can be counted in 3 beats. The bottom number, **4**, indicates the amount of time each beat occupies.

So, 3/4 time says that a measure occupies the same amount of time it would take to beat three quarter notes; 2/4 time says that a measure occupies the same amount of time it would take to beat two quarter notes; 6/8 time says that a measure occupies the same amount of time it would take to beat six eighth notes.

Remember: a measure can consist of any combination of beats and fractions of beats, so long as they add up to the number of beats indicated in the time signature.

AND TODAY?

he 20th century has seen neo-classicists, serialists, minimalists, and probably any other kind of "ist" one could think of, and there are certainly many important composers, experiments and innovations going on in the music world that are beyond the scope of this book.

Just as folk music influenced earlier composers, jazz and rock influences have played a part in the classical scene of the twentieth century (likewise, classical music has influenced this century's popular music). Sophisticated recording techniques, computers and electronics have affected the way music is composed, performed and even listened to. And "world" influences on the music scene are ensuring that classical music is no longer simply a European province, but the intellectual property of all.

A restless and revolutionary period in music, with no dominant style neatly summed up in one word, the music of the 20th century has yet to be pigeon-holed. But with or without a governing style, the story of music continues — and we shall leave the labeling of this century to the next one.

The End

Bibliography

A History of Western Music, Donald Jay Grout; W.W. Norton & Company, Inc., 1973.

Music in Time, William Mann; Harry N. Abrams, Inc., 1983.

Classic Composers, Magna Books, 1991.

Music Lovers Encyclopedia, Deems Taylor; Doubleday, 1939.

Complete Stories of the Great Operas, Milton J. Cross, Doubleday.

Chamber Music: The Growth and Practice of an Intimate Art, Homer Ulrich, Columbia University Press, 1948.

Full Orchestra, Frank Howes; Secker and Warburg, Ltd., 1942.

The Joy of Music, Leonard Bernstein; Simon and Schuster, 1959.

The Harmony Illustrated Encyclopedia of Classical Music, Peter Gammond; Harmony Books, 1989.

Elements of Music, William C. Brown Company Publishers, 1976.

Who's Afraid of Classical Music?, Michael Walsh; Simon & Schuster, 1989.

The Book of Musical Anecdotes, Norman Lebrecht; The Free Press (A division of MacMillan, Inc.), 1985.

Great Composers: Beethoven, Robin May; Hamlyn Publishing Group Ltd.,1990.

The Story of One Hundred Symphonic Favorites, Paul Grabbe; Grosset & Dunlap,1940.

The Story of A Hundred Operas; Grosset & Dunlap, 1940.

Milton Cross' Encyclopedia of the Great Composers and their Music, Milton Cross and David Ewen; Doubleday & Company, Inc., 1953.

Glossary

Adagio	Slow
Allegro	Fairly Fast
Aria	Song, especially in opera or oratorio
Chamber Music	Instrumental music for small groups of players
Chord	Two or more notes of different pitch sounded together
Concerto	Orchestral composition with major part for one or two instruments
Counterpoint	Two or more melodies, interwoven (played at the same time)
Forte	Loud
Fugue	The most developed form of Counterpoint
Harmony	Blending notes of different pitch, played simultaneously—e.g. chords
Improvisation	The art of composing music spontaneously
Key	The major/minor **scale** on which a particular piece of music is based
Madrigal	A type of song for a small group of singers popular during the Renaissance
Melody	The "horizontal" progression of notes—the part you can *whistle*
Octave	The eight notes that make up any major or minor scale
Opera	A stage play—a *drama*—that is sung instead of spoken
Oratorio	Similar to an opera, but without costumes or stage action
Overture	The instrumental music that is played at the beginning of an opera
Pitch	The highness or lowness of a note
Polyphonic	Greek for 'many sounds;' music that interweaves many melodies at once
Program Music	'Descriptive' music, intended to evoke a mood or a feeling
Recitative	Dialogue in an opera that is recited (often in a songlike way) but not sung
Rhythm	The beat or pulse of a piece of music
Rondo	A musical form in which a theme is repeated (like "Row, row, row your boat")
Sonata	A composition for a solo keyboard instrument, usually in three movements
Symphony	Orchestral composition, usually of four movements, often large and complex
Toccata	A piece of keyboard music designed to test the player's finger control and touch
Virtuoso	A performer (usually an instrumentalist) of exceptional technical skill

Index